BRITISH RAILWAYS FREIGHT STEAM

BY JOHN M.C. HEALY

BRITISH RAILWAYS FREIGHT STEAM

BY JOHN M.C. HEALY

First published in 1990 by
SILVER STAR BOOKS
24 Partridge Close
Chesham
Bucks HP5 3LH

© John M. C. Healy

Printed from artwork designed by
John M. C. Healy

British Library Cataloguing in Publication Data

Healy, John M. C.
   British railways freight steam.
   1. Great Britain.   Railway freight transport services,
   history
   I. Title
   385.240941

   ISBN 1-872024-04-1

Printed in Great Britain by
The Amadeus Press Ltd, Huddersfield

CONTENTS

INTRODUCTION

The time honoured tradition of our forefathers, fathers and historians alike has always been to inform us that the railway age began in 1728, when men began making and laying "wagon ways". These wooden railed "wagon ways" were developed around coal mines and were designed to give easy access to local rivers or ports where the coal could be loaded into boats. Had it not been for the desire to ease the conveyance of coal from mines to rivers, we would not have a railway system today.

Today's railways often conjure up the image of passenger trains and the terms Inter City, Network South East, Commuter and Holiday-maker are regularly bandied about, leaving one to forget the part played by goods and freight trains. From those early years the success of the "wagon ways" was such that their number grew to about twenty by the end of the eighteenth century. During this period it was realised that goods could be transported more effectively and efficiently if the wagons were coupled together which dictated the need to make use of iron rails instead of wooden ones. Initially the wagons were pulled along the new iron rails by horses or by a long rope attached to a stationary engine at the end of an incline, though in later years it became more apparent as the trains got heavier and the price of horse fodder increased, that a new form of traction had to be found as the two existing modes were now no longer suitable.

The pioneer of the new type of traction was Richard Trevithick who designed an engine capable of moving under its own steam which hauled a coal train over the Penydaren Railway in South Wales in 1804. Ten years after, the Middleton Railway in Leeds changed over to steam and employed a rack and pinion system around the colliery it served and the engines were built by Matthew Murray closely following the specifications of Richard Trevithick's designs. Sadly Trevitihick's locomotives were failures on the whole though one survived to be purchased by Wylam Colliery in Northumberland. The engine itself was too heavy for the track but it provided a useful basis for the colliery's new "Puffing Billy" class of locomotive built by William Hedley.

A short distance away from Wylam Colliery lay Killingworth Colliery where George Stephenson was resident engineer. Seeing the success that the competition was enjoying with steam traction and the obvious benefits, George Stephenson set about creating suitable steam engines for hauling his company's coal traffic. Due to his employers owning a series of mines, this provided demand for steam engines and the opportunity for George to improve his designs. In order to ensure his position was safe as a locomotive builder, he educated his son Robert so that he would make a suitable partner and it was as a result of this that the very first steam locomotive building company was formed in 1825. In the meantime the reputation of Stephenson had earned him an appointment as engineer of the Stockton and Darlington Railway project which was put forward to enable coal to be carried from Darlington to Stockton on the Tees Estuary. This particular line had several of the hallmarks of present day railways in that it used proper locomotives and rolling stock with flangeless wheels and true rails instead of the cast iron "L" shaped plates that had been previously employed. The line was opened to the public in 1825 not only for carrying goods but for carrying passengers as well.

The inaugural run of the Stockton and Darlington railway marked the dawning of a new era as from 1825 onwards up until 1899, new main and branch railway lines sprung up all over the British Isles. By the early 1900's the railway companies were enjoying a period of relative prosperity mainly due to the fact that little serious competition existed from road and river transport. The state of the roads was described as being "The remnants of what God had left after the flood" and the journey and journey times were such that it was hard for rural communities that were inaccessible by rivers or canals to supply market towns and cities with fresh produce.

Naturally the emergence of railways had a profound benefit on the economy and this was reflected in the different types of commodities conveyed which ranged from various livestock and agricultural produce to minerals metals, machinery, newspapers and parcels. To cater for the varying types of traffic that was generated numerous companies provided their own rolling stock and sidings which were connected to main lines in addition to the wayside depots and purpose built goods stations that belonged to the railways themselves which existed prior to the First World War. These depots were supported by large teams of goods handlers and fleets of horse and carts that delivered the goods from the railhead to its destination. In order to ensure efficient use of this distribution service, the railways employed cartage agents in a number of towns and firms like Wordie's and Mutter Howie in Scotland, Joseph Nall in the north west and Carter Paterson in the south and Pickfords became household names. With an agency method the railways could offer an admirable door to door service to the customer. The success of the agency system was varied for the private operators as the private operator suffered a large degree of competition from the railway companies cartage organisations.

Up until the First World War railways had fought successfully for traffic with the inland waterways and roads. However the war changed the status quo though as the railways were heavily used to convey troops and munitions and consequently they emerged from the hostilities in rather a worn out state. During the war vast quantities of road vehicles had been built for military purposes, and when the war ceased, thousands of these were sold off cheaply and with the experience of motor vehicles that many of the ex troops had, they set themselves up as one man trucking enterprises or they joined the few early large scale road haulage firms. Initially the motor lorry had very little impact as far as stealing traffic from the railways was concerned. Seeing the potential threat to the transportation of goods by rail in the early 1920's, Sir Ralph Wedgwood the chief goods manger of the North Eastern Railway thought it prudent to expand the agency network to cover rural areas as well to fend off the increasing road competition. The revival and enhancement of the agency scheme initially paid off though eventually the railways were forced back to having their own agents and contractors as the people they had hired realised that there was more profit in carrying goods directly by road. The latter experience had been useful to the road hauliers as they had gained a first hand knowledge of the types of goods handled by the railways and who the customers were.

For the railways to compete, they would have to repair and upgrade the permanent way and build new rolling stock as the system had been worn into the ground for the war effort but the small companies who owned the lines realised that they could not finance the heavy repairs that were necessary so consequently the railways were allowed to remain in government control until 1921. During the war there had been repeated calls for Nationalisation of the industry but the then new Transport Ministry under Sir Eric Geddes had postponed this proposal and considered it not to be expedient to carry out such a programme in peacetime. Instead he formulated a plan that would not only define the powers and obligation that the railways had as far as freight traffic was concerned, but also would allow the standardisation and rationalisation of the hundred and thirty or so companies into four big concerns. This scheme was embodied in the 1921 Railways Act which took effect from the 1st January 1923 when the London Midland Scottish, London North Eastern, Southern and Great Western Railways were born.

The creation of the aptly nicknamed "Big Four" concerns meant each company possessed a larger route mileage and from the point of view of freight traffic there were considerable bonuses in that the turnaround time between regions was quicker as there were no longer so many company boundaries. However despite this improvement the "Big Four" realised that they had to become involved with road as well as rail haulage to give an all round service that would be more impressive than that offered by private road hauliers. To this effect a series of four private acts of Parliament were passed in 1928 which made it possible if the railways so desired to carry their goods without it ever seeing the inside of a rail wagon. With the coming of the "Big Four", other benefits existed for freight traffic in that with pooled financial and technical resources, each company was able to build better workhorses that could haul heavier loads and longer trains. For the heaviest goods traffic, the grouping companies created large fleets of eight coupled locomotives with 0-8-0 and 2-8-0 wheel arrangements on which there were variations such as the 4-8-0 and 0-8-2 types designed for working the hump yards.

Whilst the engine design improved and the various classes could haul longer and heavier trains, problems existed in the actual running of goods trains. Apart from Railway internal user vehicles and goods wagons most of the rolling stock was privately owned. At the time of the First World War 60% of the wagon mileage had been running empty though with hostilities and the need for a common user policy this was reduced to 20% but it was worth noting this economic strategy only took place through necessity. A further complication with the private wagon fleet was that it in the main consisted of seven and ten ton handbraked wagons making freight operation inefficient. As a result of this a number of attempts were made to introduce a standard twelve ton wagon but many restrictions such as the capacity of cranes, hoists and lengths of sidings caused it to be abandoned.

However despite the idiosyncrasies existing in the wagon fleet that was inherited by the grouping companies, several advances had been made since 1907 to effect proper control over freight trains. The former Midland Railway had introduced this central supervision to reduce staff overtime working. A central office was established at Derby which had a jurisdiction over several district control stations. The system had a marked effect as it meant that the allocation and distribution of goods wagons was more efficient, pilot and shunting locomotives could be sought and sent for duties in other areas if available and it meant that signal routing could be planned in advance for any train. The schemes revolutionary success meant it was rapidly expanded all over the railway network. However administrative work was still required on a large scale to record the comings and goings of empty and loaded wagons.

Besides the improvement in control of freight traffic in the years of the "Big Four" reorganised the complex movements that went on in marshalling yards and the development of the hump yard evolved. This meant that wagons were propelled to the summit of a hump and then sorted by destination and left to drop down into their appropriate siding by gravity. Various refinements were made to this system with the introduction of railway brakes firstly, to check the speed of wagons. This prevented the need for shunters to risk life and limb as they ran alongside the wagons to apply the apply the brakes. At first the wagon brakes were applied by the signalmen in the control towers but as time went on electronic sensors operated them.

Sadly, although numerous improvements were carried out to various aspects of freight operation, nothing was done to modernise the wagon braking systems. Nearly all the wagons up until Nationalisation of the railways in 1948 were handbraked and these had to be pinned down individually before descending gradients which was time consuming. The other drawback was that the whole train had to rely solely upon the braking force of the locomotive and brake van, so the driver had to apply a considerable skill when running downhill or slowing down. The lack of attention to the braking problem and the maintenance of the private owner wagon status hampered railways to the extent that road competition developed even further. Hauliers also benefitted from the 1933 Road and Rail Traffic Act which although giving railways more freedom in their role as a common carrier, nevertheless allowed truck drivers to tender for goods by undercutting the rates the railways were obliged to charge. This effectively meant that in many cases lorries were carrying goods that had formerly been conveyed on the railways and the railways were left to carry unprofitable loads. This imbalance was unjust as the road hauliers were allowed to be selective and carry only the most profitable goods while the railways had to convey any commodity they were offered thus fulfilling their role as a common carrier.

Around the same time that the Road and Rail Traffic Act came into force, the railways were in the throes of revamping the whole collection and delivery service and concentrating it on railheads. This system was first made available to larger towns where precedents had been set up by large manufacturers who had established depots from where their goods were then distributed. These commodities included biscuits, foodstuffs, confectionery, livestock, fertilisers, textiles, boots and shoes. Later the railhead concept was extended to rural towns and villages where farmers and local traders benefitted. The railheads made the goods offices at wayside stations redundant but the centralisation of distribution made railway freight transportation more economic. By 1938 there was a network of some eight three railheads which covered five hundred and forty two stations which served some three thousand villages and towns.

As the road hauliers began applying for licences by the score, so railways became more bitterly opposed to them especially in circumstances where they were competing for traffic that had always been rail handled or where they were vying for trade in areas where the railways offered a better service. Finally the "Big Four" railway companies launched a simultaneous attack on Parliament demanding a fairer deal and their point was hammered home by the distribution of over two million booklets to households around the country entitled "Clear The Lines" which endeavoured to put forward their case to the general public. The latter course of action was effective enough to be able to make the government of 1939 agree to the railways charging appropriate rates for the freight they had to convey under the "Carriers Acts", but legislation could not be introduced immediately as war broke out before the next session of Parliament. This untimely intervention caused the postponement of the amendments to the carriers acts until 1953 by which time lorry traffic was enjoying a bonanza as far as growth was concerned.

During the Second World War the decline in freight traffic on the railways was halted due to the needs of the Ministry of Supply and the Army and all available goods wagons and railway routes were employed to almost breaking point. In addition to the heavy usage of railways many more lorries and vans were constructed for military purposes and at the end of the war these, just like the ones in the First World War were disposed of to hauliers which encouraged the post war lorry boom. To combat the impact of this, the railways elected to introduce a system which made good use of road vehicles for the collection and delivery of goods. Under this new method many stations had the role of receiving centres. Goods would then be conveyed to a sub railhead where they would be sorted into wagonloads which were then dispatched to a major railhead where they were attached to other wagons and then taken to their destinations. If a wagonload could not be made up or goods were unable to go straight to their destination then they were transported by a trunk motor lorry. The "Zonal" system as it was known had a considerable effect on the handling of small quantities of freight traffic in that it allowed an improvement in speed and efficiency and made operations more economical.

The introduction of the "Zonal" system was the last measure to be implemented on freight traffic by the "Big Four" companies who had introduced some 258 zones prior to Nationalisation. The latter was mainly decided upon as being the best course of action because the Second World War had caused the ravaging and wearing down of the railway system. Eventually on 1st January 1948 the London Midland Scottish, London North Eastern, Great Western and Southern Railways all became state controlled as a result of Clement Atlee's Transport Act of 1947.

Upon Nationalisation of the "Big Four" Companies British Railways inherited the largest and most comprehensive fleet of road vehicles and the most comprehensive cartage service in the world. The vehicles ranged from the little three wheeled electric powered mechanical horses to all types of petrol and diesel engined vans and lorries. Prior to the absorbtion of this fleet by British Railways the four old companies had begun streamlining their fleet of vehicles to reduce the number of different spares that had to be stocked and also this eased maintenance generally. British Railways continued this policy of standardisation as well as adding to the fleet with new more modern vehicles. At the peak of operation when the "Zonal" System was fully developed some fifteen thousand lorries, vans, mechanical horses and tractors were employed carrying nearly twenty million tons of goods and one hundred and fifty million parcels per year. Additionally railway agents and hired contractors carried further million tons of goods and some six million tons of parcels.

Despite the vast improvements which took place on the railway system in general at Nationalisation, as far as freight was concerned, although the railways had by that stage been put on an equal footing with road hauliers their role as Britain's major freight carrier was to last less than twenty years more. Over this period however the state owned British Railways did actually begin building new fleets of wagons and freight locomotives the most famous of which were the 9F class 2-10-0's. This book chronicles various aspects of the transport of goods and the associated facilities that were provided for operations between 1947 to 1967 when British Railways Freight was under steam.

John M.C. Healy

The Nationalisation of Britain's Railways is less than a month away as London Midland Scottish Railway 8f heavy freight locomotive No 8453 shunts prior to hauling a fully laden train of General Merchandise away from Cheltenham L.M.S sidings in December 1947. The locomotive later became No 48543 under British Railways and was given a black livery with red and white lining.

(Courtesy D. Montgomery)

Still proudly displaying its old London Midland Scottish Railway livery 8f class No 8469 later to become British Railways 48469 storms along through Bishops Cleeve at 6.15p.m on the 6th April 1948 with a heavily laden iron ore train.

(Courtesy D. Montgomery)

Between the bleak and barren Pennine Hills still wearing its old and rather shabby livery ex London Midland Scottish class 8f locomotive No 8532 built by the London North Eastern Railway works a block train of high sided coal wagons near Woodhead on a bright summer evening in August 1948. Note the new looking electrification masts which were part of the London North Eastern Railway's Manchester Sheffield and Wath route modernisation.   (D.J. Montgomery)

7p Jubilee Class No 45669 Fisher thunders along past Lichfield Trent Valley station with a Willesden to Crewe Parcels train.   (E.S. Russell)

The date is April 1949 as ex London Midland Scottish class 8f No 8017 trundles along at Skelton Junction with a hopper train carrying minerals for I.C.I.

(D. Montgomery)

On 7th July 1949 7p Jubilee class No 5661 Vernon heads a Leeds to Manchester mineral train near Sowerby Bridge. The locomotive later became No 45661 but when this view was taken only the tender had been decked out in early British Railways livery.

(D. Montgomery)

Ex London Midland Scottish Railway 8f class No 8089 having had its lettering from the tender and the numbers from the cabside removed so that it can be reliveried in British Railways style, it is seen here passing Cheadle station on 2nd June 1949 with a train of large hoppers for the areas I.C.I factory.

(D. Montgomery)

Sometimes it was more convenient for the railways to run goods and passenger traffic together as seen in this August 1949 view where 7p Jubilee class No 5555 Quebec heads a couple of cattle trucks and three passenger coaches near Rugeley on a Rugby Midland to Stafford stopping train. (D. Montgomery)

On 5th August 1949, former London Midland Scottish Railway class 3f 0-6-0 No 43510 is about to pass the Neilsons Sidings Signalbox with a Toton to Brent coal train. (D. Montgomery)

7p Jubilee class No 5687 Neptune rushes under the bridge carrying the upper part of Lichfield Trent Valley station on 9th August 1949 with a vacuum brake fitted train of vans and containers. (Courtesy D. Montgomery)

22xx class 0-6-0 2203 based at Stratford Upon Avon shed is seen taking a leisurely stroll southwards down the former Great Western/Great Central line with a single mineral wagon which is being returned to Old Oak Common on the 25th March 1950.   (B. Brooksbank)

Ex London Midland Scottish Railway 7p Jubilee Class 4-6-0 No 45654 Hood storms along past Standish Junction Wigan on 1st June 1950 with a south-bound van train full of general merchandise and parcels.   (J. Davenport)

On 22nd July 1950, Stanier 8f class No 48556 coasts along near Shrewsbury with a train of fully laden coal wagons. (D. Montgomery)

The date is August 1950 as a 6p Jubilee class No 45686 St. Vincent in early British Railways livery thunders through Watford Junction with a Crewe to London Euston parcels and newspaper service. (D. Montgomery)

Gloucester based engine class 3f 0-6-0 No 43258 heads gently past Tramway Junction with a coal train and one general merchandise van bound for Birmingham on 30th June 1951.   (D. Montgomery)

Saltley based 4f class No 44538 thunders past the goods yard of Royston and Notton station with an up main line coal train from Leeds to Birmingham on 24th July 1951.   (D. Montgomery)

Making light work of it an 8f class No 48331 draws a typical early British Railways mixed goods train along near Ambergate on 24th May 1952. Note the variety of different wagons that made up the train. (W. Potter)

Having retired from main line work vintage ex London North Western Railway class 2f 0-6-0 No 58328 finds itself useful shunting wagons at Crewe works on 17th May 1952. (D. Montgomery)

One of the ubiquitous 8f class No 48686 is seen passing through Foleshill on a Coventry to Nuneaton coal empties train in January 1953.   (D. Montgomery)

other train of empty coal wagons headed by class 5mt No 42761 rushes through Castle Bromwich station on a bright Summers day in 1953 on its way back to Leicestershire.   (D. Montgomery)

On the Great Central London Extension line a class 01 No 63596 effortlessly steams along near Aylestone on the outskirts of Leicester with a motley rake of mineral empties for Hotchley Hill Gypsum Works on 7th June 1953.

(John F. Clay)

Drawing past the carriage sidings to the south of Leicester London Road Station, an 8f class 2-8-0 No 48490 is seen gathering speed as she heads south with a coal train on the 2nd May 1954.

(Mike Marston)

Ex Great Western Railway 7800 Manor class No 7818 Granville Manor simmers gently as it waits the right away near Tyseley with a mixed freight train on 30th October 1954.

(D. Montgomery)

Accrington based class 7p 4-6-0 Jubilee No 45706 Express and an unidentified class 5 pound away from Leeds City station with a parcels train for Liverpool on an overcast day in June 1955.

(D. Montgomery)

On many an occasion for reasons of efficiency wagons were often attached to local or stopping services and here 7p class Jubilee No 45581 Bihar and Orissa waits to leave Ripon on 8th May 1955 with a mixed train formed of a ventilated van and three Gresley Blood and Custard liveried coaches.

(D. Montgomery)

Heading towards Grimsby, an 04/1 "Tiny" class 2-8-0 No 63601 makes light work of its train of one box van and a rake of mineral wagons. The engine was later preserved and can now be seen at Dinting.

(J.F. Clay)

During a quiet moment at Bangor station on a Summers day in 1955, much to the delight of two spotters, a class 5mt 4-6-0 No 45403 trundles through the centre road with an Afon Wen to Llandudno Junction cattle train.

(D. Montgomery)

At Marsh Lane cutting on the Great Central south of Leicester by the entrance to the city's goods depot, a class 9F No 92086 makes its way past a train of mineral wagon empties with the Abbey Lane to Fawley oil tank working.

(J.F. Clay)

Another 9f class on the Great Central main line No 92076 heads an up Annesley to Woodford Halse "Windcutter" freight near Aylestone in September 1955.
(D. Montgomery)

4f Class 0-6-0 No 43976 leans gently as it passes Wellingborough Midland station on a down mixed freight. Note the varied selection of wagons making up the train giving ample proof that at one time all but the kitchen sink was delivered by rail.
(D. Montgomery)

Vintage 1890 built 2p class 2-4-2 tank engine No 50752 simmers gently in one of the bays at Normanton station with a short parcels train on an overcast day in 1956.   (D. Montgomery)

On 8th July 1956 near Sowerby Bridge, Patriot Class 7p No's 45531 Sir Frederick Harrison and 45543 Home Guard, head northwards with a Manchester Victoria to Bradford parcels.   (Courtesy D. Montgomery)

5mt class 2-6-0 No 42757 with the minimum of effort draws a train of mineral wagons and vans past a deserted Apperley and Rawdon station on the Leeds to Carlisle line on 6th August 1956. (D. Montgomery)

Having just passed a Manchester bound mixed goods train entering Milfo Tunnel, 5mt Class 2-6-0 No 42874 heads away from the Peak Distr towards Duffield with a heavily laden train carrying a great variety general merchandise and farm machinery. (D. Montgomer

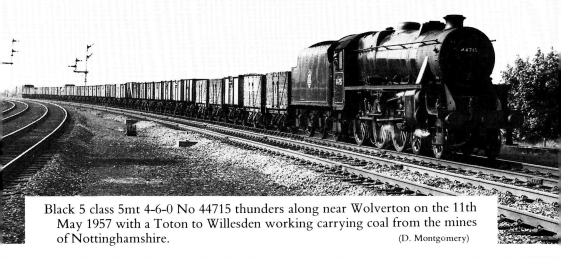

Black 5 class 5mt 4-6-0 No 44715 thunders along near Wolverton on the 11th May 1957 with a Toton to Willesden working carrying coal from the mines of Nottinghamshire. (D. Montgomery)

On 19th June 1957 4f class 0-6-0 No 44054 hauls one of the more profitable workings of the time the block coal train away from Chinley on the down slow line. The freight yard on the right was used very frequently for the division and remarshalling of trains as Chinley was where the Derby and Sheffield lines parted company. (D. Montgomery)

On 2nd August 1957 one of the mainstay of engines on freight traffic during the last years of steam on British Railways was the 9f class and here No 92114 is seen on the up slow line here having just cleared Loughborough Midland with a Toton to Brent coal train.

(D. Montgomery)

Another member of the 9f class No 92115 on the same day is seen approaching Loughborough Midland station with a Brent to Toton coal empties working.

(D. Montgomery)

With a fully laden train of coal from the Sheffield coal fields, Royston based 8f class No 48489 charges along at the helm near Killamarsh on 14th September 1957.   (D. Montgomery)

2251 class 0-6-0 No 2274 trundles through Soho and Winson Green station with a pick up goods in late September 1957. These trains were so named because from the start to the finish of their journey they called at each station to pick up a handful of loaded wagons.   (D. Montgomery)

With a long train of coal wagons and a few covered vans 8f class No 48
draws away from Chinley North Junction with a Sheffield to Manche
working on the 19th June 1957. (D. Montgome

Whilst some gangers are busy checking the permanent way near Faring
Junction, a 5mt class No 45184 rushes along on a southbound mixed frei
train on 20th June 1957. (D. Montgome

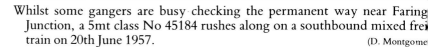

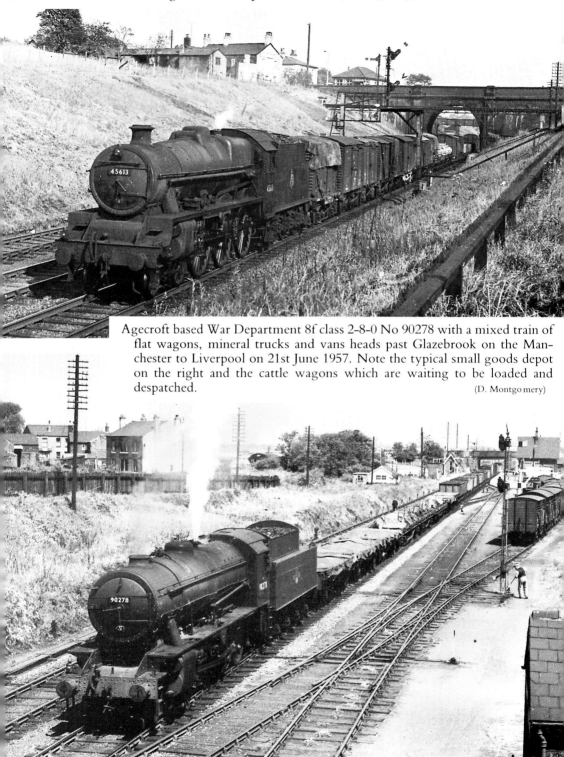

Jubilee Class No 45613 Kenya with a straight sided tender charges along past Hartford with a mixed freight on the 21st June 1957. (D. Montgomery)

Agecroft based War Department 8f class 2-8-0 No 90278 with a mixed train of flat wagons, mineral trucks and vans heads past Glazebrook on the Manchester to Liverpool on 21st June 1957. Note the typical small goods depot on the right and the cattle wagons which are waiting to be loaded and despatched. (D. Montgomery)

On the 2nd November 1957 two 3f class 0-6-0's Nos 43808 and 43766 are seen entering Hitchin station with a brick train having just left the line from Bedford Midland. (D. Montgomery)

New England based 9f class No 92044 is seen entering Hitchin station whilst working a coal train to Kings Cross on 2nd November 1957. (D. Montgomery)

7p Jubilee class No 45643 Rodney rushes through Rugeley Trent Valley station on the 9th April 1958 with a vacuum brake fitted train carrying a mixture of perishable goods, parcels and newspapers.   (D. Montgomery)

The peacefulness at the immaculately kept Churchdown station is briefly disturbed as a 4f class No 44526 saunters through with an express freight train from Birmingham for Gloucester on the 9th August 1958.   (D. Montgomery)

A mighty workhorse for a heavy load as one of the numerous 8f class No 48179 is seen passing Newton Harcourt with an up mixed freight in spring 1958. (Mike Marston)

On a snowy day in February 1959, 7p Jubilee class No 45578 United Provinces rushes past Wem station with a parcels train comprising of ventilated vans and passenger brake/luggage vehicles. (D. Montgomery)

On the 18th June 1959, the peace is temporarily broken at Lancaster No 3 Cabin as 6p Jubilee class No 45681 Aboukir thunders by with a fast fitted freight. (Courtesy D. Montgomery)

Newton Abbot based 6800 Grange class No 6813 Eastbury Grange is seen crossing the River Avon near Bristol Bath Road shed with a fully laden mixed goods train on the 18th June 1959. (Courtesy D. Montgomery)

Pounding along near Tring on the West Coast Main Line 8f class 2-8-0 48665 is seen in charge of a Willesden to Toton coal empties train on 10th August 1959. (D. Montgome...

K1 class 2-6-0 No 62057 is seen rushing along one fine Summer evening 1959 with a mixed freight on Langley Water Troughs which lay betwe... Knebworth and Stevenage on the East Coast Main Line. (D. Montgomer...

A light load for a big girl as 7p Jubilee class 4-6-0 No 45675 Hardy ambles along with three parcels vans near Hellifield forming a Carnforth to Leeds working.
(J. Davenport)

The place is Stirling and on this particular day in 1960, the photographer has captured something on his camera for almost all railway enthusiasts. On the right is the locomotive shed and coaling stage in the background where some wagons are about to be unloaded, whilst on the left a multitude of wagons wait to be sorted and despatched to their various destinations and almost unnoticed in the centre a 6p Jubilee class No 45728 is seen thundering along the main line with a partially fitted van train.
(G.W. Sharpe)

On the 2nd May 1960 7p Jubilee class 4-6-0 No 45762 thunders along near Carnforth on an up mixed express freight train. (J. Davenport)

Returning with the empties as 6p Jubilee class 4-6-0 No 45568 Western Australia is hauling a rake of milk tankers near Kibworth North.

(M.D. Marston)

Simmering gently an ex 8f war department class 2-8-0 No 90682 waits for the
right away at Toton with a long mixed freight.　　　(Courtesy D. Montgomery)

Really mixed in the true sense of the word a further member of the Jubilee class
No 45676 Codrington saunters along the slow line near Winwick junction
with several loaded full brake parcels vehicles and vans and London Midland
Scottish Railway vintage carriage in the middle returning to Liverpool as
empty stock.　　　(J. Davenport)

A scene that has drastically changed today as the station at Whatstandwell once part of the glorious main line through the Peak District now only has a single platform which serves a truncated service to Matlock. Here 8f class 2-8-0 No 48547 heads 5p 55 freight working past the station with the minimum of effort on the 23rd June 1961.   (D.J. Montgomery)

On 7th August 1961 with superpower at the helm, in the form of 7p Jubilee class No 45636 Codrington and 4f class No 44492 coast along Micklefield Bank with a Heaton to Manchester (Red Bank) parcels train.   (M. Mitchell)

A deformed member of the 9f class, the locomotive type that was designed to be the maid of all work as far as freight traffic was concerned, is represented here by No 92026 which is seen hauling a down mixed express freight on the 24th August 1961. This engine was one of nine of the class that had been adapted to take a Franco Crosti boiler system. (D. Montgomery)

A Scottish Region Dalry Road based class 5mt 2-6-0 No 42746 rushes along south of Sanquhar with an express freight bound for Edinburgh on the 29th September 1961. (D. Montgomery)

days of steam hauled freight trains are numbered as modernisation, ectrification, and new forms of traction are beginning to appear as Birken- ead based 8f class No 48260 heads an up stopping goods service through cton Bridge on the Liverpool to Crewe line on a fine December day in 961.

(D. Montgomery)

t work for a big girl as 9f class No 92149, with a fine emission of smoke, orms along northwards near Hadley Wood on the 17th March 1962.

(D. Montgomery)

Wearing a very interesting headcode indeed that for an express passenger breakdown train this little shunter No 47642 draws through London Bri having collected a large train of wagons together which it is taking Cricklewood via the Snow Hill (South to North London) link at wh point they will be marshalled into their respective trains and despatcl accordingly.

(D. Montgome

The maids of all work as far as freight traffic was concerned in the last days of British Railways steam haulage were the 9f's and here No 92159 heads south near Sileby with an up freight on 4th June 1962 comprising of loaded tank and coal wagons.

(D. Montgomery)

With signs of modernisation and electrification clearly evident 6p Jubilee class
No 45603 Solomon Islands with a through fast train bound for Manchester.

(B. Brooksbank)

On 5th June 1962 6p Jubilee class No 45731 Perseverance heads a southbound
mixed express Carlisle to London freight near Lancaster.   (Noel A. Machell)

Struggling up the gradient of Shap Wells summit 6p Jubilee class No 45709
Implacable is very glad of some help from 4mt No 42424 which is pushing
at the rear of this Carlisle bound mixed freight train on the 16th June 1962.

(Noel A. Machell)

With a fine head of steam the photographer has captured a nice shot of 6p
Jubilee class No 45567 South Australia working an engineers train near
Easenhill on the 16th June 1962.   (J. Hyde)

On the 24th June 1962 6p Jubilee class No 45613 Kenya rushes past Bare Lane station on a Morecambe to Crewe parcels. (Noel A. Machell)

Splendid scenery and an excellent action shot as 6p Jubilee class No 45560 Prince Edward Island is seen taking a drink from Dillicar Water Troughs whilst working the 3.30pm Carlisle to London meat train on the 6th August 1962. (Noel A. Machell)

Superpower as a Black 5 5mt 4-6-0 No 45232 and a 6p Jubilee class No 47537 Atlas effortlessly wend their way along near Farnley Junction with a Heaton to Manchester (Red Bank) parcels train on the 16th August 1962. (M. Mitchell)

3F class No 43762 drawing away from Bromsgrove yard having collected its train together, with a lot of steam and leaking a bit, prepares to assault the Lickey Incline with an express southbound freight on the 18th August 1962.

(D. Montgomery)

While a train of vans is being loaded in the south bay at Peterborough North, a New England based 9f class No 92041 rushes southwards through the station with an up coal train. (D. Montgomery)

When railway stations were constructed in important locations they were given a lavish provision of platforms although some of them saw little use. In British Railways ownership as shown in this picture of Leicester Central, the underused bay facilities were very useful for the storing and loading of parcels vans. (D. Thompson)

On the 5th September 1962 6p Jubilee class No 45620 North Borneo stands in the down loop of Burton on Trent with a northbound mixed freight.

(D. Montgomery)

Having collected the goods from every station on route, Ivatt Class 2mt 2-6-2T No 41235 is seen coming off the Blaenau Ffestiniog branch at Llandudno Junction while a Diesel Multiple Unit approaches on the left with a Crewe to Holyhead working on the 7th September 1962.

(D. Montgomery)

6p Jubilee class No 45671 Prince Rupert thunders past Farrington Junction on an up mixed freight which includes a passenger vehicle on the 10th September 1962. On the right is Lostock Hall Motive Power Depot where the engine was based. (D. Montgomery)

A spot of shunting at the rear of Derby Midland Station as 4f class 0-6-0 No 44118 with what looks like a tender cover plays with a few internal user coal wagons used for carrying locomotive fuel. (D. Montgomery)

64a St. Margarets based 3f class J36 0-6-0 No 65329 quietly draws past Seafield junction whilst working a pick up freight. (D. Montgomery)

An immaculately and obviously recently outshopped 6p Jubilee class No 45552 Silver Jubilee simmers gently as she backs onto a couple of scruffy internal user mineral wagons that have were used to deliver loco coal to Crewe South depot. (D.J. Montgomery)

Shunting on shed as 8f class 2-8-0 No 48464 sits outside the wagon repair shop at Stranraer after shunting the wagons under cover. (D. Montgomery)

On the same day at the same location, another 8f has been captured by the photographer in the form of No 48390 which is at the head of a long mixed express freight train heading southwards. Note the two brand new Presflo wagons that are fifth and sixth in the train. (D. Montgomery)

On the 13th July 1963 a Fairburn 4mt Class 2-6-4T No 42185 trundles along gently near Stoneyford Junction and Langley Mill with two parcels vans on their way from Sheffield to Nottingham.   (D. Montgomery)

Speeding away from the South Yorkshire Coal fields from where it has gathered its full load of wagons, 8f class No 48161 is seen heading southwards along the Midland Route towards Beighton.   (D. Montgomery)

en the most powerful locomotives are sometimes not able to manage a gradient whilst hauling a heavy load and here 9f class 92126 and its train of iron ore for Staveley is just drawing away from the banking engine that has helped it along past Stoneyford Junction.

(D. Montgomery)

With a Crewe to Willesden "Parcels and Perishables" working a 6p Jubilee class makes light work of the load near Easenhall on the 17th July 1963.

(J. Hyde)

The date is 22nd July 1963 and in this picture the photographer has captured another member of the Jubilee class in the form of No 45623 Palestine which is at the head of the Heaton to Manchester (Red Bank) parcels train on Micklefield Bank. (M. Mitchell)

One of the Modified and ugly looking 9f's No 92029 which was one of the members of the class to be fitted with a Franco–Crosti boiler system, is seen here gently coasting through Newport High Street station. (D. Montgomery)

On the 3rd August 1963 8f class heavy freight engine No 48220 with a Brent to Toton mixed goods seen near Glendon on the Midland Main Line.

(D. Montgomery)

The most exacting feat for a locomotive was climbing a gradient and here powerful 8f class No 48643 as it heads a mixed express freight requires assistance as it ascends the notorious Lickey Incline on the 16th August 1963.

(D. Montgomery)

4f class No 44226 is seen ambling through Barnt Green station on the 16 August 1963 whilst working an up mixed express freight. Note the wago covers which were once commonplace on these workings. (D. Montgomery)

A splendid photograph showing a fine view of the City of Chester in the background with the racecourse and the railway in the foreground and in this picture the pleasant scene is briefly disturbed by the passage of 6p Jubilee class No 45581 Bihar and Orissa as it rumbles over the Dee viaduct with a Chester to Wolverhampton express freight. (D. Montgomery)

Down on the Southern Region, Class 4mt 4-6-0 No 75025 waits to depart Bere Alston with a down pick up freight on the 18th April 1964.

(D. Montgomery)

On the 25th June 1964 steam vies with diesel as an immaculate 4mt class No 43044 and later class 47 diesel No D1521 each head along with a down goods past the disused station at Naburn to the south of York. (D. Montgomery)

6p Jubilee class 4-6-0 No 45604 "Ceylon" hurries along at a regular pace whilst working a down express freight comprised of container vehicles near Hellifield on the 1st June 1964.　　　　　　　　　　　　　　　(J. Davenport)

Passing one of the many woollen mills that once existed either side of the lines connecting Lancashire and Yorkshire an 8f class No 48146 rattles past Mirfield station with an eastbound train of minerals on the 26th June 1964.

(D. Montgomery)

5mt class 2-6-0 No 42926 thunders through a deserted Newlay and Horsforth station between Leeds and Carlisle with a train of up mineral empties on the 26th June 1964. (D. Montgomery)

Near Chester on the 29th August 1964, 8f class No 48740 makes light work of its rake of petrol tankers which can be seen stretching back beyond the signal cabin in the background. (D. Montgomery)

Having slowed down to a rather leisurely pace one of the untidy looking "All Bits Combined" Southern Region Q1 class engines draws past Reading with a fast through mixed freight train on the 12th September 1964.

(D. Montgomery)

As some engineers attend to the down line an 8f class 48340 rushes along the up line at Springs Branch, Wigan on the 3rd May 1965 with a mixed freight.

(D. Montgomery)

On the 12th July 1965 6p Jubilee class No 45658 Keyes is captured by the photographer leaving Wakefield tender first whilst working an engineers train comprising of a brakevan, light duty crane and mess/tool van.

(M. Mitchell)

Between Farnley Junction and Churwell on the evening of the 17th July 1965, the photographer has captured a rather splendid picture of a doubleheaded Heaton to Manchester (Red Bank) van train.

(M. Mitchell)

As some mineral wagons in the bay in the background are being loaded with scrap metal pieces from a Bedford lorry, a 5mt class 4-6-0 No 45034 heads gently over the intricate pointwork on the outskirts of Chester with a short mixed van and container train. (D. Montgomery)

An 8f class No 48063 on a down Iron Ore train rushes past the derelict Bishops Cleeve station and Goods yard on the Cheltenham to Stratford Upon Avon line on the 4th September 1965. (D. Montgomery)

Soon steam hauled freight will be a thing of the past as the wires above this
8f class engine and its train of vans carrying perishable goods are a sign that
the age of modern electric traction is dawning. (D. Montgomery)

During a quiet moment at Wakefield Kirkgate station on the 29th February
1966, a rather grubby ex War Department 8f class 2-8-0 No 90415 on a
mixed goods waits for the signal to depart, while in one of the centre roads
an unidentified 01 class is rushing through with a fast fitted freight.

(D. Montgomery)

On the 12th April 1966, Crewe South based 8f class No 48255 is seen at Hartford Junction with a train of Hoppers. (D. Montgomery)

4mt class 2-6-4T No 80133 built at Brighton trundles through Clapham Junction station on the 30th April 1966 with a short train of parcels vans bound for Woking. (D. Montgomery)

Near Shotton Low Level station on the 30th July 1966 as a 5mt class 4-6-0 is captured on film rushing eastward with a train of tankers. (D. Montgomery)

While a recently built Brush Sulzer Type 4 diesel outshopped in the British Rail blue livery waits in the siding on the right at Hellifield, one of the old order in the form of a 6p Jubilee class No 45675 Hardy draws past with a short parcels train on the 1st March 1967. (G.W. Sharpe)

In a rather unkempt and nearing the end of its days, 4-6-2 Battle of Britain Class No 34066 Spitfire is seen trundling through Woking with a Basingstoke to Waterloo parcels train. Note that Woking goods yard has been taken up and is being converted into a car park for a new generation of commuters. (Author's Collection)

A splendid view of the elaborate goods facilities that the railway companies provided even at country stations is admirably depicted in this 1967 view of the facilities at Charlbury in Oxfordshire. (Author's Collection)

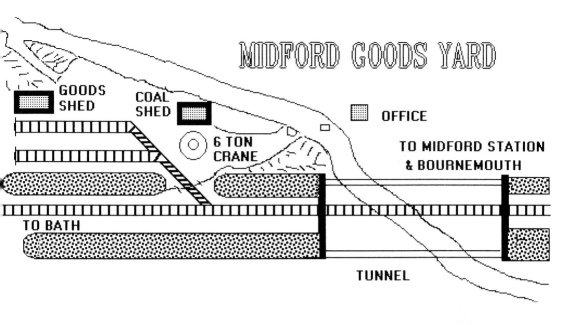

An example of two small goods yards provided on the Somerset and Dorset
Bath to Bournemouth line which served the villages of Midford and Cole.

(John. M.C. Healy)

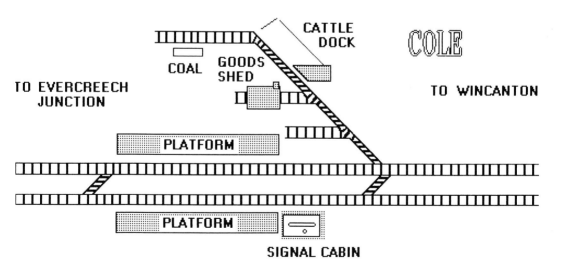

SEDBURGH

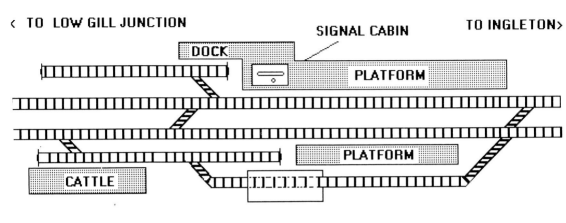

‹ TO LOW GILL JUNCTION

SIGNAL CABIN

TO INGLETON›

DOCK

PLATFORM

PLATFORM

CATTLE

GOODS SHED

Diagrams of the more elaborate facilities that the London Midland Scottish Railway Company provided to serve the towns of Sedbergh on the Ingleton to Low Gill line and Staveley on the branch from Windermere to Oxenholme.

(John. M.C. Healy)

STAVELEY

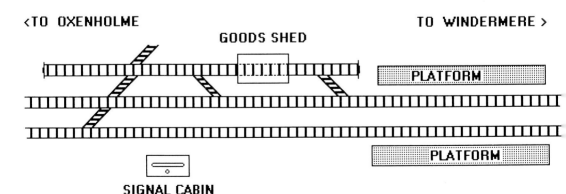

‹TO OXENHOLME

TO WINDERMERE ›

GOODS SHED

PLATFORM

PLATFORM

SIGNAL CABIN

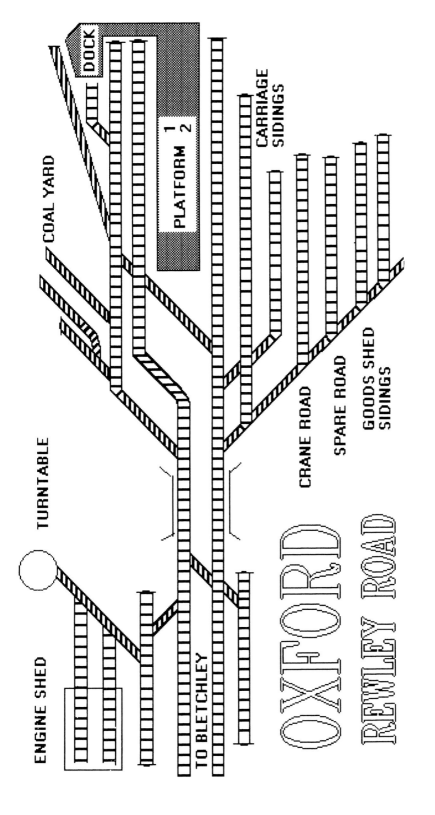

Although space was limited in cities, each railway company where possible provided a goods depot near the main station if possible as at Oxford Rewley Road.

(John. M.C. Healy)

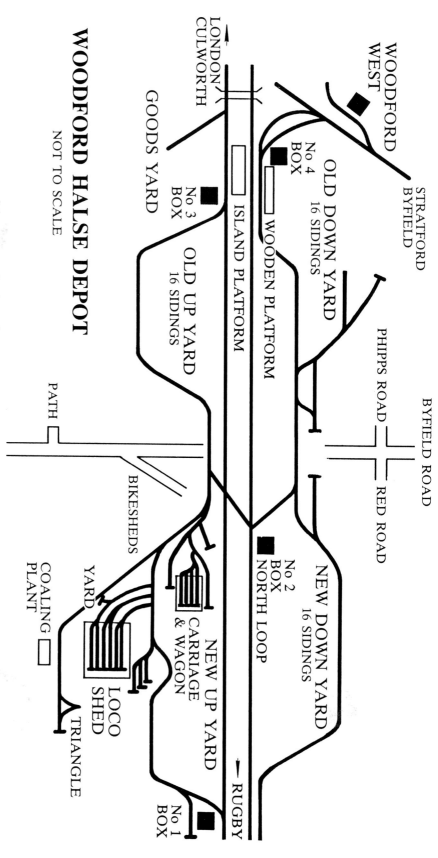

WOODFORD HALSE DEPOT

NOT TO SCALE

LONDON
CULWORTH

WOODFORD
WEST

STRATFORD
BYFIELD

GOODS YARD

No 4
BOX

OLD DOWN YARD
16 SIDINGS

WOODEN PLATFORM

No 3
BOX

ISLAND PLATFORM

PHIPPS ROAD

BYFIELD ROAD

RED ROAD

OLD UP YARD
16 SIDINGS

PATH

No 2
BOX
NORTH LOOP

NEW DOWN YARD
16 SIDINGS

BIKESHEDS

YARD

COALING
PLANT

NEW UP YARD

CARRIAGE
& WAGON

LOCO
SHED

TRIANGLE

No 1
BOX

RUGBY

At certain major interchange points on the railway network large marshalling yards and depots were built for the purposes of sorting wagons and freight and routing it to its correct destinations. Woodford Halse yards on the old Great Central main to London shown here were once described as being the "Pride of Europe" because of their handling capacity and efficiency.

(John. M.C. Healy)

An example of the time consuming art of shunting at a small goods yard with Standard class 4 No 75030 at the helm in 1966. (Courtesy M.P.C. Moorland)

The railway incline at Kilmersdon that was a typical feature at large collieries which allowed coal to be taken from the coal face to sorting sidings where wagons were sorted before being taken to their final destination over the British Railways network. (Courtesy M.P.C. Moorland)

As well as Passengers Paddington also dealt with a large amount of parcels and other freight, though it must be said that milk churns were something of a rarity at the terminus itself. The three men are engaged in the labour intensive activity of unloading a British Railways road vehicle in 1962. (P. Slater)

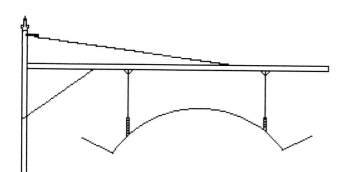

An example of a loading gauge which were once a familiar sight at many large and small goods depots, there purpose being to check the height of loaded wagons.

(John. M.C. Healy)

Old practises die hard with a couple of shunting horses at work shortly after Nationalisation of the railway system.

(Courtesy M.P.C. Moorland)

A rake of ferry wagons being loaded onto a railway wagon ship via a linking bridge. (Courtesy M.P.C. Moorland)

Shunting by the Capstan system which could be very dangerous due to the occasional errant wagons and fraying ropes. (Courtesy M.P.C. Moorland)

How transhipment was done in the old days prior to Containerisation with a small number of sacks being hoisted up from the hold ready to be loaded into waiting wagons on the dockside. (Courtesy M.P.C. Moorland)

The huge sundries goods depot at Bristol Temple Meads which has since disappeared with the large reduction in freight traffic and the remodelling of the station. (Courtesy M.P.C. Moorland)

The interior of a goods sundries depot, with parcels being sorted on a conveyor belt. According to Doctor Beeching such places were uneconomic due to the vast number of men employed in them and poor competition with the more efficient road haulage operations. (Courtesy M.P.C. Moorland)

Coal empties running through the retarders on the down hump yard in Whitemoor yard. (Courtesy M.P.C. Moorland)

Once a familiar feature on the roads and especially at stations was the Scammell "Scarab" which wore an eyecatching livery of red and cream. The version shown is the three ton vehicle seen here outside lodge road depot at Marylebone. (P. Slater)

Turning now to Marylebone where an L1 tank is slowly reversing out of the station past one of an enormous fleet of road vehicles that belonged to British Railways once a familiar sight at stations all round the country.

(P. Slater)

Made redundant a weighbridge and goods office at the remote location of Helmdon in Northamptonshire on the former Great Central London Extension. (John. M.C. Healy)

At the same location the derelict goods shed and store which survive partially intact though nature is fast engulfing the buildings. (John. M.C. Healy)

New uses are taking over but at least for the time being the former goods shed at Brackley Central is safe. At one time nearly every station in Britain had a lavish provision of buildings to handle goods traffic and their size varied according to the importance of the place they served. (John. M.C. Healy)

A splendid reminder of the size of goods handling facilities that could be found in cities round the country is portrayed by this view of the former Great Northern Railway Company's Goods Warehouse in Manchester, which fell out of use during British Railways ownership. (John. M.C. Healy)

The old goods warehouse and office at New Basford on the outskirts of Nottingham on the old Great Central line to London which was abandonned in
the mid to late 1960's.   (John. M.C. Healy)

Breakdown Train going to clear the line, or Light Engine going to assist disabled train or empty coaching stock train timed at the speed of an express.

Mixed Train or Breakdown Train not going to clear the line.

Express Freight Train or Ballast Train authorised to run at a maximum speed of 35m.p.h. Empty coaching stock not carrying group 1 headlamps.

Parcels, Newspaper, Fish, Meat, Fruit, Milk, Horses, Cattle or Perishable Goods train comprised of vacuum braked stock with brake pipe connected to the engine or Express Freight Train or Livestock, Perishable or Ballast Train with not less than one third of the vacuum braked vehicles connected to the engine.

Freight, Mineral or Ballast Train or Wagon Empties Train carrying a through load to its destination.

Express Freight, Fish, Meat, Fruit or Cattle Train. Ballast Train not running under group 3 or 4 codes or special train conveying 36 ton breakdown crane to the scene of an accident.

Through Fast Train not running under group 3, 4, or 5 codes carrying a through load.

Light Engine or Light Engines Coupled together or just an Engine and Brake Van.

Freight, Mineral or Ballast Train calling at intermediate stations.

Ballast, Freight or Inspection Train requiring to stop in between signal cabins or Branch Freight Train.

Key ★ = Lamp Position on Locomotive.
   ○ = Lamp Bracket Position.

STEAM FREIGHT FINALE

Although the domain of this book is the years 1947 to 1967, the real rot began to set in for freight traffic as long ago as 1962 with the advent of the Beeching Report which outlined proposals for the Reshaping of Britain's Railways. Beeching's argument states that in the freight field there was a large disparity between classes of traffic. Wagon loads of general merchandise, which loaded awkwardly gave rise to very little through train movement and made that kind of operation into a bad loss maker. Sundries traffic was considered unprofitable for similar reasons. The two types of freight traffics which showed the best margins overall were minerals and coal. Coal trains made a small margin of profit over full cost while mineral traffic fell just short of doing so. Additionally these are classes of freight which give rise to a higher proportion of through movement of well loaded trains than others. Besides the traffic carried by vehicles designed solely for goods Beeching reckoned that freight that went by coaching stock such as parcels and mail was also profitable.

Of the stations handling freight one third produced less than one per cent of the stations freight receipts and one half handled less than three per cent. So the total revenue derived from the least used half of the total number of stations and the cost of running them is set out below:

Receipts from: £m per annum

Originating Passenger, Parcels and other coaching train traffics
at the least used 50 per cent of all passenger stations 4.8

Freight Traffic forwarded from the least used 50 per cent of all
freight stations 1.7

Estimated cost of least used 50 per cent of all stations 9.0

From these figures for 1961 which were approximately correct it was apparent to Dr. Beeching that the revenue of all kinds of freight traffic handled at the least used 50 per cent of the stations did not match the cost of running the stations themselves. The result was that it was thought better if a high proportion of the railway system was closed.

Beeching's report delved into every kind of freight traffic which fell into four categories i.e. Sundries and General Merchandise, Parcels and Mail, Coal and Mineral. Where Mail and Parcels were concerned there was a considerable overlap because the railways and the Post Office both operated a similar service and so both services lost money. Beeching proposed that where possible the Post Office service should be integrated with the railways parcels service. The additional consideration was the closure of the unprofitable routes which would mean the reduction of the number of possible collection and delivery points but the report had a way round this with proposing that the Post Office take a more active part in serving outlying areas which would be cut off under Beeching's Reshaping of British Railways.

The most uneconomical freight operation was the transportation of general merchandise mainly because most of the traffic was sent from one station to another in single wagon loads. When the Beeching Report was compiled the railway network was made up of several main line routes which were connected to a huge series of branch lines and consequently there was hardly any distance between stations. This had mainly been done because of the unreliability and slowness of road traffic. However by the early sixties the railways had lost their advantage due to the fact that the staging of wagons between the numerous marshalling yards meant that goods traffic suffered delays which made the British Railways service unattractive. The average turn round time between loads was reckoned as being 11.9 days with the usual transit time being about one and a half to two days. Many road hauliers were able to offer same day delivery service and Beeching's aim was to encourage the development of through freight services and the abolition of the old wagon fleet which would be gradually replaced by new rolling stock. Alas when this part of the plan was put into effect much of the traffic left the railways and went by road. The main reason was not because Beeching's plan to replace the existing freight transport system was impractical but because when numerous stations and lines were closed, many companies found it more viable to take their goods direct from a to b rather than take them to the nearest railhead where they could be transported by rail and then by road to their destination.

Unlike general merchandise traffic coal movement on railways in the early 1960's was more profitable mainly because there was a lot of through train operation for the benefit of large customers. However smaller consumers still relied on delivery of individual wagon loads to stations and private sidings. The latter was part of an involved process as wagons were staged at many stops on route. Beeching was very critical of this type of operation and dictated that on a modern system if most of the coal was to be handled in train load quantities and hauled over greater distances substantial savings could be made to the cost of transportation.

Under the train-load philosophy most of the wayside stations and sidings where coal was handled by merchants disappeared and they were encouraged to travel to the new concentration depots that were established. Beechings plan advocated the creation of some two hundred and fifty depots which would cover a radius of ten miles distribution and be large enough to warrant complete mechanisation and the provision of a fleet of special purpose road vehicles for delivery to the customer. Not only did the distribution depots receive a restyling but also the operations at the origination point or colliery end. The problem for collieries lay firstly in the fact that no one of them in the early 1960's produced enough coal of any one type to supply a large customer by train-loads and secondly in their lack of storage bunkers and facilities for efficient loading. For storage collieries used to borrow wagons from the railways at no cost which would lie in sidings for sometimes two maybe three days before loading or despatch took place. Due to this archaic mode of operation the road hauliers were able to take advantage

of the revenue that coal traffic offered them as they could transport the goods much more economically.

The lack of proper static bunkers caused difficulties also for the railways because with the advent of the new large, braked, hopper wagons, which were able to carry more, operate at speed and disgorge their contents quickly their turn round time was slowed down and consequently they could not be used to the best effect. Because some of these new wagons were retained by collieries before the installation of proper bunkers, British Railways imposed heavy charges for the privilege.

In Dr. Beeching's opinion, the most profitable type of goods transported was mineral traffic because the vast majority of it was carried in block trains and these comprised of large rakes of modern wagons that served efficient terminals which yielded large profits to the railways and passed on only minimal costs to the customers. Not all mineral traffic was conveyed in block trains as some by its very nature had little justification for being moved in other than the traditional wagon loads and quantities concerned were not enough to make up train loads of one commodity. The smaller loads of freight led Dr. Beeching to examine in detail the contribution that various types of minerals made to the overall freight traffic that the railways carried and their suitability for railway haulage from the point of view of terminal conditions, size of consignment, loadability and length of haul.

The terminal conditions of mineral traffic fell into some ten categories and flowed on a road to road, road to station, road to dock, road to siding, station to station, station to dock, dock to dock, station to siding, siding to dock and siding to siding basis. Only the latter siding to siding movement was profitable as the direct costs far outweighed the receipts on the other nine types of flow. The main reason that only the siding to siding traffic was very profitable was due to no costly vehicle to vehicle transfer being required. In a few of the categories such as station to station, station to dock and siding to dock haulage only small losses were incurred and the questions raised at the time were whether the traffic could be profitable in the future, whether all the traffic had to be carried and how much could be saved if the traffic was totally withdrawn.

Much of the direct costs incurred in railway transportation came through road collection and delivery, terminal expenses, trip working, marshalling, provision of wagons, trunk haulage and administration. The theory in Dr. Beechings report was that if most of the unprofitable traffic was withdrawn and small terminals which gave rise to unnecessary expenditure were closed, large scale savings would be made. In circumstances where traffic had to be maintained for customers efforts had to be put into streamlining operations. The streamlining referred to the larger terminals where services and staff were reduced to meet the new level of traffic that was handled by them. For the smaller terminal though the rearrangement or proportional rationalisation meant certain doom as the amount of freight left after such measures would hardly justify their retention. Although the railways had an obligation to carry all types of goods, the Beeching policy dictated the removal of all loss making traffic unless there was scope for making improvements to the

old wagon load haulage system. Removal of the unprofitable services according to Beeching would cause little harm to the main core of mineral traffic as profitable workings mainly used the larger terminals and therefore the customer would be little inconvenienced. The people who were hardest hit were merchants and traders who had established businesses in station yards that served small town and country communities. However the changes to the system meant that instead of going to the local small railhead all collections had to be taken further afield to a large railhead. In actual fact with the disappearance of the small railheads it wasn't long before many companies and road hauliers discovered that it was quicker for goods to do the whole journey by road rather than rail.

To make up for the lost traffic that would be axed by the Beeching recommendations, a series of publicity campaigns were started to encourage any potential siding to siding traffic which was revealed to be profitable, especially if it could be conveyed by block or liner trains. The liner trains took over much of the small siding traffic that ran from siding to siding or from siding to dock. Where siding to station and siding to road traffic was concerned only that which moved in large flows between cities and towns was designated as being suitable for liners. More or less the same principle was applied to the other categories of traffic mentioned earlier with the proviso that if the goods were not suitable for block or liner trains then higher charges should be raised to stop that particular kind of goods moving by rail.

The liner train was designed to allow proper integration between road and rail haulage to allow large flows of traffic carrying a mass of small consignments previously moved by the wagon load to travel over medium and long distances at low cost because of being part of an economical through train operation. The biggest economy lay in the transfer from road to rail as under the old system goods had to be picked up from their point of origin, loaded onto a railway wagon and finally unloaded and loaded onto a lorry at the other end before the final destination could be reached, all of which was costly and uneconomic but with an internationally designed container, goods were loaded at the origination point and not unloaded again until their arrival at their destination. The other major benefit of containerisation was the ability to transport goods in a secure environment that was free from potential theft or vandalism.

With the advent of liner traffic, the door to door traffic costs were reduced to below what road hauliers charged and administration requirements were drastically pruned. Due to the astonishing revelation that container trains could transport goods more cheaply than road hauliers, Beeching reckoned that a further sixteen million tons of road borne traffic could be attracted to the railways and distributed between the fifty five envisaged terminals.

As far as the railways were concerned, one of the most awkward types of traffic was the conveyance of sundries or freight which was in too small a quantity to be carried by the wagon load. This kind of traffic was vastly uneconomic for the railways as a large number of road vehicles and much manpower was needed to offer the customer a comprehensive service. By the early 1960's some of the sundries traffic drifted away from the railways as lorry drivers took advantage of being able to offer a better service in some areas. The latter was allowed to happen because the railways had maintained a system where too many terminals handled too little traffic and so movement of through trains was scarcely possible. In some cases vans or wagons would travel on a journey only partly loaded or alternatively they would be carried in similar fashion and then transhipped several times during journeys.

Due to the poor nature of the sundries operation, Beeching progressively reduced the number of depots handling this kind of traffic to some one hundred, as well as removing all the unnecessary light loading, transhipment and accompanying administration work. Those depots that were subjected to heavy modernisation required massive capital outlay spending on them to knock them into shape but even after this the sundries traffic did not present an attractive picture as far as profit and loss was concerned. Like mineral traffic the only hope for making the cartage of sundries profitable lay in the liner trains which could carry sub containers or pallets where previously only part of a wagon would have been used. The sub containers and pallets were also very useful in that they made handling a lot easier at depots than it had been with goods wagons. One major obstacle in the efficient conveying of sundries traffic was the need for the railways to maintain a massive road vehicle fleet which cost some twenty two million to maintain and operate in 1961. With rising costs in labour and increases in staff wages and the general inefficiency of the road fleet, a general manager was appointed with the sole task of organising the coordination of the cartage of sundries and the reduction of the number of road vehicles.

Not only were road vehicles for the cartage of sundries subjected to a considerable reduction in number but also the wagon fleet suffered the same fate. Since the second world war due to a steady decline in rail hauled traffic the number of wagons had diminished gradually up until the early 1960's when the Beeching plan came into operation. At that juncture in 1962, the railway wagon fleet had been reduced by nearly four hundred thousand since Nationalisation in 1947. Much of that reduction took place in 1961 and 1962 though a further hundred thousand wagons had left the network by the end of 1963 mainly because of the alteration to traffic flows, the introduction of a greater amount of through working, the elimination of poor wagon utilisation at stations and on branch lines and the obsolescence of much of the stock.

By 1967, the same year as steam ceased to operate on freight trains, Beechings Report on the Reshaping of British Railways had seen nearly all of its recommendations implemented. Many route miles of freight line had disappeared along with several goods stations and private sidings which were all deemed to be unprofitable in the age of the block train and the bulk load. However in theory the report seemed to make good sense but in practice the removal of most of the small amounts of goods led to the vast increase in the number of lorries on the road which had to become larger and more powerful to cope with the increased demanded for their type of transportation. Also the pruning of the network only encouraged companies and merchants to use roads more and more as the railways became ineffective at carrying small to medium size loads. Whilst Beechings plan was good as far as economies were concerned, it didn't allow the railways to fulfil their role as a comprehensive carrier. With the amount of small quantity traffic that was carried on British Railways during the early part of the 1960's demand obviously existed for this operation which could have been made more efficient on a depot to depot basis with a great reduction in the number of staff, an improvement in handling time, mechanisation, the introduction of small wagons for special traffic and the use of passenger carrying units in some cases

Undoubtedly the period 1947-1967 was one of the most fascinating eras in the history of British Railways in that during this time the network underwent several radical changes to make it become more efficient and competitve with rival road transport.